A Beginner's Guide To
Bettas

Written By
W.L. Whitern

Contents

© 1986 by T.F.H. Publications, Inc. Distributed in the UNITED STATES by T.F.H. Publications, Inc., 211 West Sylvania Avenue, Neptune City, NJ 07753; in CANADA by H & L Pet Supplies Inc., 27 Kingston Crescent, Kitchener, Ontario N2B 2T6; Rolf C. Hagen Ltd., 3225 Sartelon Street, Montreal 382 Quebec; in CANADA to the Book Trade by Macmillan of Canada (A Division of Canada Publishing Corporation), 164 Commander Boulevard, Agincourt, Ontario M1S 3C7; in ENGLAND by T.F.H. Publications Limited, 4 Kier Park, Ascot, Berkshire SL5 7DS; in AUSTRALIA AND THE SOUTH PACIFIC by T.F.H. (Australia) Pty. Ltd., Box 149, Brookvale 2100 N.S.W., Australia; in NEW ZEALAND by Ross Haines & Son, Ltd., 18 Monmouth Street, Grey Lynn, Auckland 2 New Zealand; in SINGAPORE AND MALAYSIA by MPH Distributors (S) Pte., Ltd., 601 Sims Drive, #03/07/21, Singapore 1438; in the PHILIPPINES by Bio-Research, 5 Lippay Street, San Lorenzo Village, Makati Rizal; in SOUTH AFRICA by Multipet Pty. Ltd., 30 Turners Avenue, Durban 4001. Published by T.F.H. Publications, Inc. Manufactured in the United States of America by T.F.H. Publications, Inc.

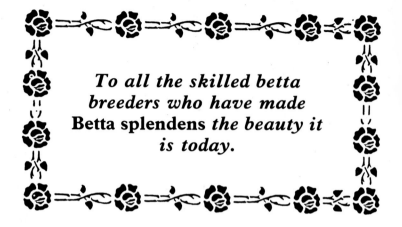

To all the skilled betta breeders who have made **Betta splendens** *the beauty it is today.*

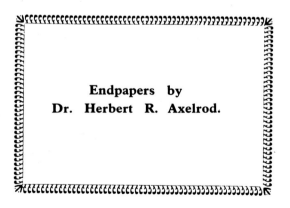

Endpapers by Dr. Herbert R. Axelrod.

1.
Introduction

In the aquarium hobby, popularity is often fleeting. Many are the species of fishes that have been imported, enjoyed a short vogue, and then drifted out of the picture to be seen again only rarely. This is not true of the

This magnificent gold betta clearly illustrates the grace and beauty of the cultivated Betta splendens *today. Photo by Andre Roth.*

little Asiatic fish known to aquarists as *Betta splendens*, the Siamese fighting fish or just plain betta. Bettas have been kept and enjoyed by hobbyists almost from the earliest days of the hobby, and there is every indication that they will always retain their favored status.

It is odd that a fish with the temperament of the Siamese fighting fish should have achieved such prominence in the hobby. As its common name suggests *Betta splendens* is no angel. Males of the species will fight with one another almost to the death, and even females can be nasty, especially to their sisters. But although this unhappy trait would seem to put a damper on any hobbyist's enthusiasm for bettas, it doesn't, because the fish has a characteristic far outweighing the disadvantage presented by its pugnacious nature: it is beautiful.

Two male bettas go at it with fin and fang, presenting a picture of color and action. Photo by Gene Wolfsheimer.

A beautiful blue male courts his somber-hued mate with spread fins and gill covers. The betta is one of the easier aquarium fishes to both keep and breed and has long been popular with hobbyists.

Our present-day Siamese fighters owe their beauty to the breeders who devoted their lives to changing the drab wild bettas into today's long-finned, multihued jewels. This transition was accomplished over the course of a century and is the product of patience and meticulous attention to detail. And a hard job it was, for our current stocks of Siamese fighting fish bear little resemblance to their ancestors. Gone are the fish of murky greenish brown coloring and stubby, graceless fins; in their place we now have brilliant fish with flowing fins of imperial carriage.

In their native waters in Thailand, where the betta's natural animosity toward other males of his species is often put to practical use through the medium of staged fishfights on which considerable sums are wagered, *Betta splendens* lives in rice paddies and other sluggish waters. Many hobbyists might surmise from this that bettas are able to stand the most deplorable water conditions. Unfortunately, this is not so. Although the fish can do with considerably less space than other species, other conditions must be met, especially in the area of temperature maintenance. This need for higher than average temperatures is particularly important if an attempt at spawning is undertaken. This is usually the case, because most aquarists who have kept bettas with any degree of success make a stab at breeding them for two reasons: raising the fry presents a challenge, and the resulting new crop of fish can be sold for a good price, thus defraying at least part of the hobbyist's expenses.

Now that we've met *Betta splendens* in general, let's go on and study him in more detail.

2.
Vital Statistics

ORDER: Percomorphi

SUB ORDER: Anabantoidea (fishes with air-breathing accessory organs)

Here's looking at you! This splendid red male betta has come a long way from the drab wild bettas of the rice paddies of Thailand! Photo by Dr. Herbert R. Axelrod.

A gold male carefully tends his bubblenest containing eggs. This specimen displays especially long and graceful finnage. Photo by H.J. Richter.

This female Betta *splendens* displays more bright color than is the norm for the female of the species. Female bettas are relatively unaggressive, but may fight among themselves. Photo by Michael Gilroy.

FAMILY:	Belontiidae (labyrinth fishes)
GENUS:	*Betta*
SPECIES:	*splendens*
AUTHOR:	Regan, 1909
COMMON NAME:	Siamese fighting fish, betta
RANGE:	Thailand
TEMPERAMENT:	Males are very aggressive and vicious to other males of their own species, but they may be maintained singly in a community aquarium; females usually are peaceful and several may be maintained together provided there is no male in the same aquarium, but some females are bullies.

TEMPERATURE RANGE	70° to 85°F; optimum 78F.
MATURE SIZES:	Males 2½ to 3 inches; females slightly smaller
SEX DIFFERENCES:	Males have the more exotic color patterns, enhanced by the large draping finnage.
VARIETIES:	There are today many separate color varieties of bettas, including red, blue, green, and combinations of these colors. There are even albino and all-black bettas. However, all varieties require substantially the same treatment; they differ mainly in their genetic color properties and their appeal to the individual hobbyist.

This brightly-colored, oddly-patterned betta is a "sport" that was collected in the wild.

3.
Water Conditions

Siamese fighting fish are anabantoids. All fishes within this group of families can survive in water that has a low concentration of dissolved oxygen, because they are equipped with air-breathing accessory organs that per-

A wide variety of quality aquarium maintenance products are available that will help the beginning aquarist keep water quality up to par! Photo by Vince Serbin.

A beautiful cellophane betta with transparent fins cruises about its attractively planted aquarium. The species does best at a water temperature of about 78°F. Photo by Dr. E. Schmidt.

mit air to be taken directly from above the surface of the water. This air is taken in at the mouth and passed to the air-breathing accessory organ known as the "labyrinth". Because this air-breathing accessory organ is designated as a "labyrinth," anabantoids are often referred to as the labyrinths or labyrinth fishes. Bettas absorb very little dissolved oxygen from the water, being more dependent on the accessory organ than most species within this group.

Many aquarists have a misguided idea that any of the labyrinths may be introduced into an overcrowded aquarium because they can get their oxygen from the air and will not deplete the supply of dissolved oxygen in the water. This practice is worse than poor: it can even be fatal.

To maintain bettas in an active and full color state, they must be maintained in water that has a slightly higher temperature than heat normally used for other species. A temperature of 78°F. is ideal, but even this should be a few degrees higher for spawning purposes.

At temperatures between 68° and 72°F., bettas appear to be listless, do not surface as often, and their color pattern and fin-spreading are less conspicuous. These colder temperatures react upon the fish's metabolism to such an extent that a state of semi-dormancy is induced.

Without exception, labyrinth fishes are seen to best advantage if maintained in a fairly large aquarium. Bettas will acclimate themselves to smaller surroundings, but they look prettier in a big tank.

Although only one male betta should be maintained in an aquarium, several females may safely be placed together in community aquarium. Of course, there should be no male present in such an aquarium. Females, although not as strikingly beautiful as the males, do have very interesting color patterns and will enhance any tank. Of all the anabantoid fishes, bettas undoubtedly are the most exotic and in the greatest demand by all aquarists.

Success in maintaining any fish in captivity is dependent upon several general factors not the least of which is the provision of correct water conditions. Bettas are no exception to the general rule, and when they appear listless, fail to display fully extended fins, or show less vivid color patterns, it must be assumed that something is wrong. We have already seen that temperature plays an important part in the well-being of the betta. Two other factors, directly related to the chemical composition of the water, play almost equally important roles. These two factors are the hardness of the water and the

This male displays shorter, more rounded fins than some of the fancier strains but is still a beautiful sight with its intriguing fin pattern. Photo by H.J. Richter.

A cornflower blue male shows nearly perfect fins. The betta will not show itself to best advantage unless water conditions are to its liking.

pH of the water. Water hardness can be defined generally as the amount of dissolved minerals, especially calcium, in any given quantity of water. The pH of water is dependent upon its concentration of hydrogen ions. In short, pH is a measure of water's acid or alkaline properties. On the pH scale, values of less than 7.0 are acid and above 7.0 are alkaline; 7.0 is neutral, neither acid nor alkaline.

Before attempting to provide the correct water conditions there should be some assessment and appreciation of the water conditions under which wild bettas live. Bettas are native to waters that have a soft muddy bottom, a condition prevalent in the rice paddies that they inhabit. This indicates that their home waters would be murky and of an amber tinge. It would also be very soft and would not exceed eight degrees of hardness and positively would not have any saline content. It would also be slightly acid but would not be lower than 6.8 pH.

To provide these conditions is not difficult. Soft water (8 DH is considered fairly soft) can be acquired by using demineralized or distilled water in 50% proportion with normal tap-water or well-water. The acidity and amber tinge can be achieved by suspending a small bag of peat moss in one corner of the aquarium.

There are available at any pet store testing kits for water, both for pH and DH. Each includes full instructions as to its method of operation; they are fairly accurate.

Although bettas can withstand some minor abuses due to incorrect water conditions, it will definitely affect their general deportment and later may interfere with their breeding potential. Thus the preparation and maintenance of correct water conditions is of prime importance. Healthy, active and colorful fish can be maintained only when correct water conditions are provided.

A gorgeous red betta, with the pale yellow "Cambodia" body color. This fish was doubtless the result of careful attention to proper diet, water conditions, and disease prevention.

4.
Feeding

Many of the problems that arise, including diseases, can be traced to a lack of understanding in relation to the great importance of supplying correct foods and feeding procedures. It is essential that aquarists should endeavor

A pair of male Libby bettas in combat. The fish in the foreground has torn a piece of fin from his rival and angrily chews on it. Fins, however, are not an advisable part of the betta diet! Photo by Dr. Herbert R. Axelrod.

to acquaint themselves with the foods indigenous to the fish's native habitat. If there is a preponderance of live animal foods available in these areas, then it is important that every endeavor should be made to duplicate these food conditions. Often this requires that some elements of their food should be supplemented with substitutes.

Bettas are carnivorous, and this indicates that animal life and finely scraped raw meats should constitute the majority of their diet. In their native waters, mosquito larvae are in plentiful supply at all times. The same live food is readily available to the hobbyist throughout the summer months, but it must be substituted for during the winter months. Frozen mosquito larvae are available

Mosquito larvae—high on the list of favorite betta foods. The larvae can be collected in the wild during the warmer months or purchased frozen in the winter. Photo by Michael Gilroy.

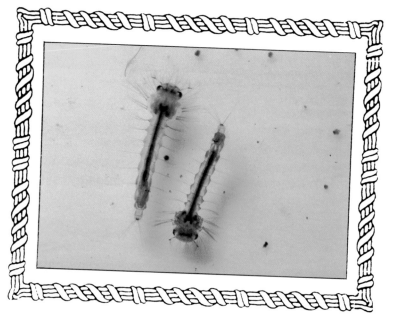

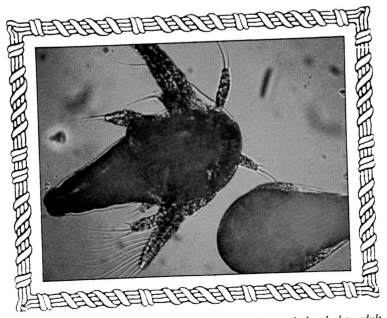

Newly hatched brine shrimp nauplii. Artemia, *from the newly-hatched to adult* *sizes, is particularly good betta food and can be fed in either live or frozen form.* Photo by Charles O. Masters.

during this period of the year. An excellent substitute can be readily supplied by finely chopped small red garden worms, white worms, or newly hatched brine shrimp. The brine shrimp are particularly good. Bettas will accept any of the commercially prepared dry foods, but it is best to supplement these with the type of foods already recommended.

When conditioning bettas for breeding, diet scheduling is very important. As they have very strong teeth, although their alimentary tract is shorter than in other fishes of comparable size, they are equipped to accept finely scraped meats. These should be in the raw state and fed quite frequently.

It is very important for aquarists to experiment for a few days with specific types of foods; careful observation should enable the hobbyist to determine which foods are most suitable.

Care must be taken to assure that over-feeding does not take place. Uneaten foods quickly decompose and foul the water to an extent that may be dangerous. Foul water harbors unwanted bacterial colonies that may be the direct or secondary cause of many of the internal fish diseases. Such diseases do not readily respond to medication. Time devoted to preparing proper feeding schedules and diets containing a high nutritive value is well spent. It can be instrumental in avoiding unnecessary problems.

Bloodworms are an excellent and increasingly popular live food for all smaller, carnivorous fishes, bettas included. They can be purchased live, frozen, or freeze-dried. Photo by Michael Gilroy.

5.
Diseases

Maintaining fish in a healthy condition should always be of prime consideration. This is far more simple than trying to effect a cure for a diseased fish, because many diseases are neither readily detected nor readily medi-

Maintaining a disease-free aquarium environment will assure the hobbyist that his fish will look like this near-perfect red male betta, shown descending from its bubblenest. Photo by Rudolf Zukal.

25

A breeding pair of beautiful gold bettas begin preliminary spawning movements. Soon, they will embrace beneath the male's bubblenest, where the eggs will be expelled by the female, and fertilized and placed in the nest by the male. Photo by H.J. Richter.

Blue male betta, displaying the narrow dorsal and anal fins that are in contrast to more and more broad-finned strains. Photo by Dr. Karl Knaack.

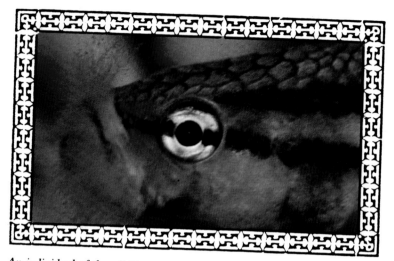

An individual of the wild betta species, B. macrostoma, *afflicted with* Saprolegnisis, *or mouth fungus. Photo by Dr. Herbert R. Axelrod.*

cated, and there is always the danger that in curing a disease there may be after-effects that have far more serious effects upon the fish than the disease itself.

Healthy fish are quite capable of withstanding many diseases through natural resistance, but when they are in poor health this resistance is lowered. Far too often bettas suffer from malnutrition induced by improper feeding schedules and poor quality foods.

Many diseases require several days to develop before presenting any visible signs. Aquarists should always make a careful daily observation of their fishes. If any suddenly display unusual behavior, sores, wounds, or darkened areas on the body, they should be immediately isolated into a separate aquarium. Daily observations will detect any further developments. Once the symptoms are sufficiently clear to permit the disease to be diagnosed, immediate treatment and medication should be given.

There are available today many commercially prepared medicants, including the antibiotics. The use of these should be approached discreetly because of possible complications later. Undoubtedly many of these medicants will effect a cure, but fishes, like people, can build up a resistance to antibiotics. This indicates that with a repetition of any disease the medicant would be non-effective or at least less effective.

There is also a general belief, not yet fully proven, that many drugs have a definite effect upon the reproductive organs. This is indicated by a deterioration of the stock derived from spawnings. In some instances they appear to be much smaller and are fewer in number.

It is never advisable to hurry a cure for any disease; many diseases have a specific time cycle, and the application of additional medicants will not hurry the cure.

A tail-less betta. This condition is congenital and not the result of disease, although some drugs used in the cure of disease could have a direct effect on the reproductive organs of bettas and result in stunted or deformed fry. Photo by Mervin F. Roberts.

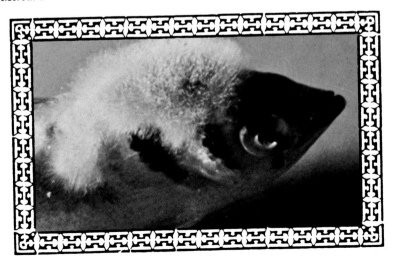

Pastel mint-green betta, displaying the Cambodian color pattern, with green iridescence. Photo by James Sonnier.

A marvelous red male betta, showing the scalloped, or combtail, edge of the cau-
dal fin. Photo by B. Kahl.

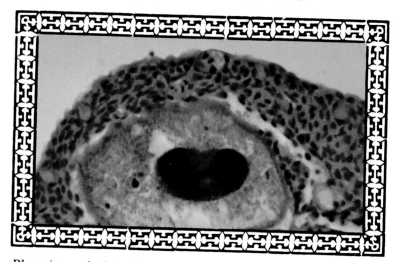

Photomicrograph of the ich parasite embedded in the skin of a fish. After a period of metamorphosis, the parasite leaves the host's body as a cyst, which sinks to the bottom to incubate and release the young. Photo by Dr. Sylvan Cohen.

Furthermore, it is dangerous to use larger dosages than those prescribed for any given medicant. Many medicants contain ingredients that are harmless if used as prescribed, but dosages in excess of the prescribed amount may be lethal.

In many instances, either disease or wounds are of such proportions that any attempt to medicate is useless. It is more humane to destroy an infected fish under such conditions.

Never gamble with disease; if it strikes an aquarium and is contagious, remove all fish immediately and place them into isolation, separating those that have visual symptoms of disease into another aquarium. The aquarium from which the diseased fish have been removed should be stripped down. The sand or gravel should be sterilized by pouring boiling hot water over it. The

THE WORLD'S LARGEST SELECTION OF PET, ANIMAL, AND MUSIC BOOKS.

F.H. Publications publishes more than 900 books covering many hobby aspects (dogs, cats, birds, fish, small animals, music, etc.). Whether you are a beginner or an advanced hobbyist you will find exactly what you're looking for among our complete listing of books. For a free catalog fill out the form on the other side of this page and mail it today.

. CATS . . .

. . . BIRDS . .

. . . ANIMALS . . .

. . . DOGS . . .

. . FISH . . .

. . . MUSIC . . .

For more than 30 years, *Tropical Fish Hobbyist* has been the source of accurate, up-to-the-minute, and fascinating information on every facet of the aquarium hobby.

Join the more than 50,000 devoted readers worldwide who wouldn't miss a single issue.

plants should be sterilized by immersion in an alum solution, and any rocks or driftwood should be treated in a similar manner. The aquarium should be thoroughly sterilized with a strong salt solution.

To the more serious aquarist, additional equipment such as a small microscope, a good magnifying glass, and a small set of scales is invaluable. Many fine specimens can be cured of a disease provided the necessary equipment and medicants are immediately available. Delay will often cause the disease to spread to such proportions that medication fails to be effective. Here are some common betta ailments and their description and cure.

White Spot (*Ichthyophthirius*). Every aquarist at some time or other has had to face the problem of clearing up an aquarium containing fish having this disease. Gener-

A barb showing a very heavy infestation of the Oodinium *parasite. Any disease should be detected and treated at an early stage, and not allowed to progress to this point.*

ally the accepted theory for the cause is stress from a sudden drop in the water temperature. To some extent this is correct in the majority of infections, but fish in a state of malnutrition will also be readily susceptible to the same disease.

The first visual indication of its presence is the appearance of small white spots; these spots usually show first on the fins, later on the body. Each of these spots indicates that the responsible parasite—*Ichthyophthirius*—has penetrated through the fish's skin into the tissue. Actually, the infection takes place several days prior to the appearance of the white spots, but about five days are usually required for the parasite to go through this first stage. This is known as the stage of "metamorphosis," in which the parasite passes through a complete change of appearance and condition.

After this period, the new form leaves the body as a hard-cased cyst. Upon leaving its host, the cyst slowly sinks to the bottom of the aquarium, lodging on any obstacle it may come in contact with on the way.

The period of incubation within these cysts is approximately five days, after which they burst open, releasing several hundred perfectly formed and active young parasites.

There are several recommended medications for effecting a cure: methylene blue, strong common salt solutions, and the many commercially prepared medicants. These latter include some of the wonder drugs or antibiotics. Be sure to follow directions on the package. Undoubtedly they do effect a cure, but caution should be exercised in their use. Very little is known of the actual after-effects, particularly in relation to breeding potential.

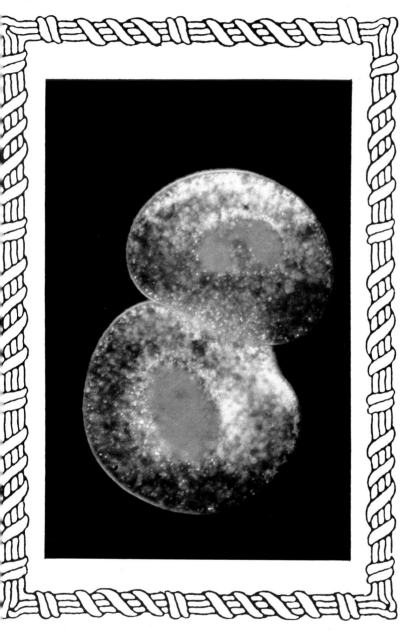

Ichthyophthirius multifiliis, *the causative agent of "ich," or white spot disease, photographed under high magnification during cell division. Photo by Dr. H. Reichenbach-Klinke.*

A paradise fish, Macropodus opercularis, *in the early stages of disease, probably velvet (oodinium). If your betta displays such signs as clamped fins or discoloration, diagnose and treat the disease quickly. Photo by Rudolf Zukal.*

From the viewpoint of safety, use a pet shop medication containing quinine hydrochlorate. This is easily available. The standard dose is 5 grains for each ten gallons of water in the infected aquarium. If no appreciable change is seen after three days, the same dosage can be repeated without any harmful effects upon the fish. When all white spots have disappeared from the infected fish, add 2 drops of 2% Mercurochrome to each gallon of water. This will destroy any of the parasites remaining in the infected aquraium. Allow one day for complete medication, then remove 50% of the water, replacing with fresh tap water. It is very important that not more than two drops per gallon of the Mercurochrome are used or it may cause distress to the fish. This medicant has toxic properties if used in too large a dose.

Velvet Disease *(Oodinium)*. Bettas are very susceptible to this disease, in common with most other Asiatic species.

The first indication of velvet is the appearance of a yellowish fuzz slightly below the dorsal fin. This spreads rapidly until the whole of the back becomes covered. Medications for velvet can be bought at any pet shop.

At one time many experts advised the use of five pennies to each gallon of water in the infected aquarium. Their theory was that the copper in the pennies set up a reaction with the acids in the aquarium water. This produces small quantities of dissolved copper salts that were lethal to the parasite responsible for this disease.

A severe infestation of the fungus Saprolegnia *in a male guppy. At this point, the victim is beyond the hope of recovery. Photo courtesy N. Nolard Tintigner.*

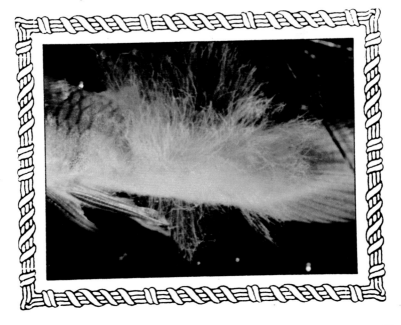

A Cambodia red and white butterfly betta in full display. This fish shows an almost perfect fin pattern and shape. Photo by Al Liebertrau.

A wild-type male betta on a mission of egg retrieval during spawning. A descending egg can be seen just above the fish's dorsal fin. Photo by H.J. Richter.

Another method was to get two pieces of copper sheeting around 1½ inches square and attach an insulated wire to each. One piece was placed at each end of the aquarium and the wires were attached to a 4-volt dry cell battery, permitting the current to pass through the aquarium water for several hours. There are no recorded instances in relation to the after-effects of this medication or whether or not it effected a permanent cure.

Fungus *(Saprolegnia)*. Any fish infected with this disease should be considered to be in a secondary stage of infection. This fungus will show itself on the outer edges of any wounds that have been acquired through fighting or hitting against a jagged rock. Whenever a fish, particularly a betta, suffers a wound, the wound should be treated immediately to prevent fungus. Antifungal agents and fungicides are available at your pet shop.

Finally, it is always beneficial to remember an excellent old adage—never give disease a place to start. This can be assured by maintaining clean aquaria and providing properly scheduled feedings of foods that have the necessary nutritive values to keep fish in a healthy state. When fish are healthy they can easily resist many diseases, except those that are hereditary.

6.
Breeding

Bettas, like many other anabantoids, are bubble-nest builders. When the eggs are laid, they are picked up by the male and deposited under a nest composed of floating sticky bubbles. While there, they are carefully

The sight every betta keeper waits for—a pair locked in a spawning embrace beneath a beautifully constructed bubblenest! Photo by H.J. Richter.

tended by the male. It is not difficult to induce bettas to spawn; the hard part is raising the fry. Fry of most anabantoids are very small and are consequently hard to feed. In addition, they are tender and require special precautions on the part of the hobbyist, especially in regard to temperature fluctuations.

Before an attempt is made to spawn bettas, there are a number of factors that must be considered, and every effort must be made to implement as many of them as can be undertaken in a practical manner.

For success, certain points must be given careful consideration. Among these points are:

The Aquarium

This should be a minimum of ten gallons in capacity. It should be thoroughly sterilized with a strong salt solu-

This intriguing view of spawning bettas, taken from below, shows the fish circling each other prior to the nuptial embrace. Photo by Hilmar Hansen, Aquarium Berlin.

Closeup of betta fry hovering just below the bubblenest. The young remain in the nest for three or four days, closely tended by the watchful male. Photo by H.J. Richter.

tion and should have a tight-fitting full hood to prevent cold drafts from blowing across the surface of the water. This is exceedingly important, as will be detailed later.

Plants and Planting Arrangements

The selection of plants should be considered from the viewpoint of affording a hiding place for the female, because the courtship of bettas is usually aggressive and more often than not, vicious. Suitable hiding places for the female may include several bunches of cabomba (*Cabomba caroliniana*) or ambulia (*Limnophila* species). The small fronds of these plants are also used by the male to help support the bubble-nest and prevent its breakup. The best arrangement is to plant densely in the two back corners.

Sand or Gravel

It is best not to use sand or gravel in the betta spawning tank, because it is easier for the male to see eggs that

A photograph of an unusual event, a mating between a male betta and a female paradise fish, Macropodus cupanus dayi. The pair was kept alone in a spawning tank, and after a few false starts, spawned in the normal anabantoid manner. Photo by H.J. Richter.

The male of the betta-paradise fish spawning pair dives to retrieve the eggs before they reach the substrate. In this case, the eggs hatched into well-developed fry, but they failed to survive into the free swimming period. Photo by H.J. Richter.

Closeup of a betta's bubblenest, anchored to the leaves of Salvinia *and duck-weed. The mass of opaque white objects in the center of the nest are the eggs.*

have fallen to the bottom if no such material is present. Also, absence of foreign elements in the tank further reduces chances for the presence of unwanted organisms.

Water Conditions

Extreme care should be exercised in the preparation of the water, because on this depends whether or not the attempt will be successful. The pH should be 6.8 (slightly acid) and not more than 8 degrees of hardness. It is recommended that about 50% distilled or demineralized water and ordinary tap water should be used.

Filtration and Aeration

This is necessary but should not be constant or too strong. The home waters of Siamese fighting fish do not

The male of a spawning pair of bettas is caught just in the act of snatching a falling egg after spawning. He will place it among the bubbles of the nest, before resuming spawning. Photo by H. J. Richter.

The opaque globules in this photo are the eggs in a betta nest. The eggs are heavier than water and would sink if they did not adhere to the nest's bubbles. Photo by Gene Lucas.

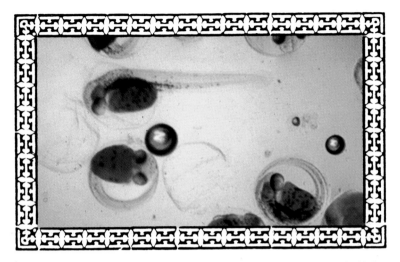

Betta fry developing within the eggs. The eggs will not develop properly if they sink to the bottom of the tank; it is not known whether this is due to the need for oxygen or the reduced pressure at the surface. Photo by Gene Lucas.

have the turbulence that can be created when forceful filtration or aeration is employed. Try to arrange filtration or aeration on an intermittent basis, preferably two hours on and four hours off.

Breeding Temperature

Although from 80° to 85°F. is a proper spawning range, the most suitable temperature is an exact 80F. This must be maintained constantly, and this situation demands the use of a thermostatically controlled heater.

Conditioning Breeding Pair

Two weeks prior to spawning a pair of bettas, careful selection should be made. Special attention should be paid to the size and color pattern; the female should be well rounded on the ventral side, indicating she is full of ova.

A pair of gold bettas in a spawning embrace. The eggs are descending and the male is turning quickly to retrieve them. Photo by H. J. Richter.

The male gold betta tightly embraces his mate during spawning. The female will normally expel between one and 15 eggs during each embrace. Photo by H. J. Richter.

For a few days there should be a glass divider in the aquarium. Once the breeding pair have been placed, one on each side of the partition, daily observation should be made. Once the male spreads his fins, usually followed immediately by the building of the bubble-nest, the glass divider should be removed.

The male will intermittently pay attention to building the bubble-nest or chasing the female. In the actual spawning act the male will wrap himself around the female, and she will release from one to 15 eggs. Simultaneously, the male releases sperm. As each batch of eggs is released the male catches them in his mouth and places them in the nest.

The full spawning period usually is around two to three hours, and upon completion the female should be removed. Often she is in a battered state, with badly torn fins or bitten gill plates. She should be placed into a separate small aquarium where she will have time to recuperate.

An adventurous young betta cruises about beneath its bubblenest.

Male betta tending his brood. During this period, the hobbyist must guard against cold draughts reaching the water's surface as the developing labyrinth organs of the fry could be damaged, with fatal results.

At this stage it is advisable to feed some type of live food to the male during the period he is attending the bubble-nest. A well-fed male is not inclined to become cannibalistic.

The eggs usually hatch within 48 hours, but the fry do not leave the nest until the yolk sac containing their initial nourishment is absorbed. This usually requires from three to four days, after which the fry become free-swimming. They will remain constantly at the surface, and any that sink are immediately picked up by the male and replaced at the surface.

During this stage of development the young fry need plenty of food, and microorganisms should be provided in abundance. At an age of about two weeks the fry commence to develop the air-breathing accessory organ, the labyrinth. This development requires at least five days.

It is during this period that most aquarists experience heavy losses, mainly because they fail to guard against cold drafts reaching the water's surface. Every effort must be made to assure that the air immediately above the water remains at the same temperature as the water. The slightest amount of colder air passing over the surface causes the developing labyrinth to become clogged with mucus. If this happens, the fry die almost immediately.

Far too often less than 10% of a spawning is successfully brought to maturity. This can be traced to lack of special attention during the period the labyrinth is developing. Once the young fry have successfully passed this period of development, they should continue growing and reach maturity.

When the fry reach an age of between three and four months, the males should be removed to individual containers. These can be either one-gallon glass jars or, preferably, small 2½-gallon tanks.

Feeding Young Fry

For the first two weeks after the fry become free-swimming there should be available quantities of infusoria. To avoid fouling the water, do not feed too much at one time. It is recommended that three tablespoonfuls daily should be added to the water. This should be supplemented with a few drops several times daily of a solution containing powdered yeast. This solution is excellent for promoting continued propagation in the

Male betta at the nest. Bettas will spawn every two weeks when in good condition, but idealy they should be allowed to breed only every six weeks. Photo by H. J. Richter.

This beautiful red male shows a richness of color and a symmetry of fin shape that would make him highly desirable as both a breeder and a show fish. Photo by Dr. Karl Knaack.

Most female bettas are "nothing to write home about" where it comes to color, but this white-faced emerald green fish shows an extension of dark green throughout the body that makes it both rare and desirable. Photo by Al Liebetrau.

aquarium water of microscopic animal life greatly needed by the growing young fry.

When the young fry have reached an age of two weeks, newly hatched brine shrimp and finely chopped white worms may be introduced into their feeding schedule. Finely ground commercially prepared dry foods may also be offered at this time.

For sturdy growth and excellent body formation and color pattern, a daily feeding of finely scraped raw chicken liver should be given. Controlled experiments have proven that young fry fed this daily develop much faster and are more robust.

Finally, from the time the young fry are free-swimming there should be a small feeding of extremely fine dry food. This feeding should be placed into the aquarium just before retiring for the night. Young fish require a constant supply of food. Very often, failure to realize this causes heavy losses, mainly from starvation.

Decrease of Water Depth in the Aquaruim

The usual practice for breeding any of the anabantoids, and bettas are no exception, is to fill the breeding aquarium only half way. In a ten-gallon aquarium this would amount to a depth of approximately 6 inches.

The reason for this is that the young fry when first hatched remain constantly at the surface. However, some of the weaker ones will gradually sink to the bottom. These are usually spotted by the attending male and quickly picked up in his mouth and replaced at the surface. Very often some of the young fry sink unnoticed and because of the water pressure are unable to regain the surface.

Once the fry have reached an age of one month, additional water should be added, but only in very small amounts. An excellent method is to mark one of the posts of the aquarium, on the outside, with black lines one quarter of an inch apart. Commence these markings at the surface of the water already in the aquarium.

This additional water must be of exactly the same quality and chemistry as that in the aquarium. To assure this, it is advisable to prepare this additional water well ahead of the time it is to be used.

Do not pour this additional water into the aquarium; it should be added very slowly. The best method to attain this is to use a very narrow siphon much smaller in diameter than the normal plastic air line hose. The required amount of additional water should be added not more frequently than every four days.

Spawning Periods

Bettas will spawn, when in good condition, every two weeks, but this should not be permitted. Such frequent spawning can only result in weakened fish that fail to develop to their full color and size.

Breeding pairs of bettas should be conditioned and permitted to spawn not less than a month or six weeks between spawnings.

Improvement through Breeding

Many aquarists have experienced bitter disappointments, particularly from the first spawning of bettas. Usually the young fry lack the brilliance of the parents and more often than not fail to develop to the same size.

This factor is more pronounced when two color strains are crossed. Those experiencing this situation should not be discouraged, because bettas require at least three generations before they show their full coloration and in many instances their normal size. Because of this factor extreme patience is required.

Very often in a batch of young there may be one or two that have distinct differences in color pattern or only slight variations. These should be developed and brought to maturity, and if it so happens that there are both males and females, they should be bred. The resultant young fry from such a mating should be closely observed for any further changes in color pattern. It must be remembered that it requires many generations before a new color pattern can be bred to a true likeness of its parents. Because of this factor many aquarists, upon observing the results of their first successful spawning, become disappointed and disillusioned, thinking that their effort has not been successful. Others feel that perhaps they have commenced with inferior stock or that it is not worth the effort because of the ultimate results.

Many of these situations would not possibly happen in nature, but when breeding is undertaken in captivity there are many factors missing, and although some may be duplicated in the home aquarium, those that are lacking may be the direct cause for the disappointment.

Actually, breeding fishes is not just a matter of placing a pair together. It is the results of the mating and the possible potential it provides that count. There is little interest in breeding just for the sake of propagating a species. It is the development from this initial effort that provided the incentive from which is derived the interest one expects when undertaking any hobby.

Suggested Reading

ENETICS FOR THE AQUARIST
y Dr. J. Schroder
BN 0-87666-461-3
FH PS-656

ontents: How To Keep Breeding Records.
he Pure Line. Mendel's First And Second
aws. Sex-Linked Inheritance. Interaction
f Non-Allelomorphic Genes. Exchange Of
enes Between Chromosomes. Founders Of
enetics. Mendel's Third Law. Polygenic
heritance. Polygenic Sex Determination.
elanism And Mottling In The Mollies. In-
mpatibility Of Germ-Cells In The In-
eritance Of Fin Abnormalities And With
espect To The Color Gene "Fuligonosus."
he Action Of Suppressor Genes In The
erlin Guppy. Harmful Effects Of Genes
rom Different Species. Inheritance In
odes Of Behavior. Variations Of
henotype.
oft cover, 5½ x 8", 125 pages
0 black and white photos, 59 color photos,
0 line drawings, 12 tables

ALL ABOUT BETTAS
By Walt Maurus
ISBN 0-87666-783-3
TFH PS-654

Contents: What Is A Betta? Keeping Bettas.
Spawning Bettas. Raising The Fry. Buying
Bettas. Genetics Of Today's Bettas. Raising
Bettas For Fun And Profit. Judging Bettas.
Index.
Audience: This book is designed to be of
great value to hobbyists of all degrees of experience who are interested in keeping bettas
and in learning about the many new color
and finnage varieties that have been
developed in the recent past. A specialized
book about a very popular fish, the Siamese
fighting fish. Ages 13 and over.
Hard cover, 5½ x 8", 128 pages
26 black and white photos, 51 color photos,
15 line drawings